A

A Prose Poem

Annie Petrie-Sauter

Bright Hill Press
At Hand Chapbook

Treadwell, New York

A Plastic Bag of Red Cells
A Prose Poem by Annie Petrie-Sauter

At Hand Poetry Chapbook Series, No. 31
Book Design: Bertha Rogers
Cover Art: Annie Petrie-Sauter
Editor in Chief: Bertha Rogers
Editorial Assistant: Lawrence E. Shaw

Library of Congress Cataloging-in-Publication Data

Petrie-Sauter, Annie.
A plastic bag of red cells : a prose poem / by Annie Petrie-Sauter.
p. cm. -- (At hand poetry chapbook series ; no. 32)
ISBN 978-1-892471-61-1 (alk. paper)
I. Title. II. Series.

PS3616.E8665P63 2010
811'.6--dc22

2010026485

A Plastic Bag of Red Cells is published by Bright Hill Press, Inc., a not-for-profit 501 (c) (3) literary and educational organization founded in 1992. The organization is registered with the New York State Department of State, Office of Charities Registration. Publication of *A Plastic Bag of Red Cells* is made possible, in part, with public funds from the Literature Program of the New York State Council of the Arts, a State Agency.

Editorial Address: Bright Hill Press, Inc., 94 Church Street, POB 193, Treadwell, NY 13846-0193; Voice: 607-829-5055; Fax: 607-829-5054; Website: www.brighthillpress.org; E-mail:wordthur@stny.rr.com

Contents

For the Street

And for Paul

1.
Outside the Church

Outside the Church

The clinic hardly ever called the cops
The church never did   as it stood above
The measured doses
Of free penicillin and Quell
Above those eternally seeking
Salvation
In the all-night rap rooms
Soaking abscesses   in patience   in stupor
In confusion
And hot water

Up against the church

Between the gray
Walls and the low branches
You had to crawl
Like a penitente over the roots
Ducking beneath the leaves
To get to the sanctuary
Empty spray cans and garbage   a comic
Book altar
  of the abandoned
Clothes
And the discarded rags
Of the gold paint huffers

Glittery and stiff
Raggedy beds unrolled
You could lie there and watch
The all-night squad cars turn the corner
Their lights barely penetrating
The thick California evergreens

Nobody entered here uninvited
Even during the four months of rain
This place was almost dry
Except for the endemic

piss puke blood

But you couldn't just bring someone here
Like you could to the triangle between
  Telegraph and Dwight Way
Or to the little park where they tore down the
  building
Or to Ho Chi Minh
This place was Sacred Ground

A Place Unseen

Unless you were one of those so inclined to
See it. In the mornings, between card tricks,
Wake-ups, and the first polite wine vomit

Of the day

It was the most pleasant place on earth.

Sitting in the dirt   reading   sewing
Counting change   or fucking somebody

Who will always love you
even if you turn out to live in another
body
or if each of you acquires another face
another personality   another name
another life   or being

Even then   you know they
will always love you
Reading Tarzan together
with nowhere to go
Napping in the dirt
As close to God as I ever came
outside the church

2.
Pilgrim Thanksgiving (Leftovers): Pardee Street (maybe 1974 or ’5)

Pilgrim Thanksgiving (Leftovers): Pardee Street (maybe 1974 or '5)

You gotta understand
That outside—was a space
About a foot and a half wide,
Where only the windows looked
Out.
It was in that space
that the hooves went by.
Upside down.
Four of them.
Bobbing and weaving—
about eye level.
Underneath—where you couldn't see them,
Were the two drunks
Who accounted for the somewhat less than
graceful movements
Of the deer.

The deer itself?
Was dead.
Hit and run up in the Hills:
Pinole.
The drunks had taken the beast up there
To drop off their Run-Away Chicks,

Hey, it was Thanksgiving—
So the 14- and 15-year-old Run-Away chicks?

Command-performance-at-home.

The rest of us?
Were home. We lived here.
Pardee St. Leftovers.
Except for Jake and Joe—
They were working construction
For Saint Anthony: quintessential
Patron Contractor of the Lost—
They'd panhandled him.
"Get a job," he'd answered.
"Hire us," they'd said (he had).
So now, they—Run-Away Chicks and the rest
Of the wino crew,
Lived there. BJ's
Crashing at the site.
BJ's garage
Up on The Ave.

Last year, Before Delaney had left, For The East,
Silver had been fine.

Delaney swore it—Silver had been fine.
Then, when she came back?
        She jess' found her like this.
Ya know, running around the old beat-up
  bungalow
In calico aprons—taking in "boarders."
Jeeze?—Boarders?
People calling her, "Mrs. Butts?"
But, now? No denying it
Silver was fucked up.
She just sat there—
In the middle of the floor
Stoned out of her mind—
Burnt out—
On way too much
Domestic bliss.

Slowly, disaffectedly, dripping
Chocolate milk
Down her baby's head.

Delaney was back.
Come in on the bus—on Monday?
Sleeping on a workbench
Set up in the old slug room—
So named for the other residents—

The slugs, like ordinary drunks,
Were transients
Who nightly came up
From The Mayonnaise Bar—

Jar *lids* of beer
Silently they crawled,
Oozing between the cracked floor boards,
Marking their direction with slimy neon
trails—

Yellow-Green-Glowing,
Fluorescent,

They mapped the floor
To their own, personal
Somewheres.

Anyway,
Delaney had taken the workbench.
Chili, her brother,
As Rip-Stop-Tight as a security fence,
had slept on the floor,
Sleeping bag pulled tight around his face—
Only his nose exposed.

The wood stove cranked in the next room.
A cozy Thanksgiving morning.
The turkey was cooking—
Red-Neck-Tom,
—Recently released from the joint—
Had been up early—popped it in.
In truth?
He hadn't been sleeping much anyway—
On-account 'a the witches—you know
The ones?
Those chicks? The ones he had been living
with
When
He first got out?

You know, the ones who were
shrinking
his penis In his sleep, of course—
Well?   What?

Hey, he had already lost a few inches.
"Anyone know a counter-spell?"
He muttered to the turkey.

Jake and Joe dumped the deer out back
On a rusty ringer washer,

Still spinning.

Delaney woke up.
She went searching for some air.
There was the deer.
She puked.

"Hi honey, I'm home, and I brung dinner,"
said Jake.
"Hey, let's get this sucker done up."
He passed out.

Joe went out to gut and skin it himself.
One of the three doors in the house opened.
Out from her own
Personal boarder-space came

A Viva,

"The infamous boarder, herself."
"A boarder?"

She had on slippers.
Boarders. Slippers.

No one really knew what that meant.

Shit, No one even really owned this place.
Delaney was the only one had been there
when they had made the deal.
$875 down and $84 a month to Golden West
Mortgage,
But still, that was less than one AFDC.
And, from the looks of it?
They had at least one AFDC
And two, maybe, three genuine SSIs.

Fact was—People just lived there.

Viva was still lucid, because it was
still early.
She shuffled to the stove, poured
a cup of coffee.
She sat at the table
Muttering.

Delaney, Joe and Jake, had,
Apparently, insulted Mr. Butts.
"Mr. Fucking Butts?"
Who the hell was he kidding? Demanding
Viva call him that?
"Mr. Butts? Harry, AKA Sparky, known
street loser rip off?

Now he was also, apparently,
Silver's new old Man?

Explains some things about Silver,
Delaney thought.

Viva got out all her little bottles
and neatly lined up the pills
Around the Bottom of her cup.
One by one, she plucked them like
berries;
And ate them.
Haldol-antidote
Stelazine-antidote
Thorozine-antidote
Soon, she just sat and stared.

Jake came to about the time that Viva left
The planet
For the day.
Jake sat down beside her.

Eyes rolling with no particular
direction.
Just rolling—Looking like a mix
of Howdy Doody,

Maybe some Custer—A dash of James Dean?
She didn't know.

He tried to speak,
But then he passed out again. Muttering in a stupor.
"Hey. You."
"Sweet thing. . . ." He stammered.
"Hey. You an' me, baby. I, I got the plan.
You got the goods—Wanna share?"

Viva answered in an antipsychotic-monotone.

"Would Mr. Butts Approve? No. He is master in this house,"

She said. Knowingly.

(Well, as knowingly as anyone on three separate anti-psychotics can ever know
Anything. Ever.)

Sensing that he wasn't getting over,
Jake slid in closer.

"Sweet thing, sweet thing,
I know what's going on here. . . there's
  bucks, that's what.
Bucks to be made here. So listen, Sweet
thing . . . about the bucks". . . . He passed.
Out.

Chin smacking the edge of the
  beautiful

Hexagonal
Table top that in some other life,
Kenoshi the potter had painstakingly
  crafted.
Now no one noticed.
Red Neck had on an apron tied in a bow
The oven door was open.
He was leaning over the turkey with a
  plastic bulb-baster.
Joe and Jesse were smoking a joint by the
  barrel woodstove
Chili was messing with his bike out front,
And Ed, well, Ed was in his chair,
Drinking a beer.
Silver? Macy had shown up, and
Harry had told River, "Clean up the kid,"

as he had ducked
Into the bedroom with Macy.

Delaney came back into the kitchen and
Surveyed the scene; one long look—
Grabbed a screwdriver,
A hatchet, a hacksaw. . . .
Shit! Even bloody deer was better than
this.
She grabbed a still-warm beer as she
passed by the fridge.

Slam.

Out the back screen door.
Outside, Delaney hammered the carcass.
She wondered?
Was Jake just so fucked up that he couldn't
see that Viva was a freaky space Cadet?
Or? Maybe was he so strung out on the
booze that he couldn't see what was
happening?
Or?
Or. (Pause.) Oh, she thought.
(She was getting a little clearer with each
whack)—

It began to dawn on her—. No maybes
about it.
He was just so fucked up—
All the time
That he just didn't care?

Whoa.
Now, that is really an attractive
quality,

She thought (Not kidding)—but just the
same

Pissed that she had missed it.

She snapped out of it.
Grabbed a leg.
Pried at the joint with the point of the
screwdriver, getting more and more
Agitated.
In the end she just hauled off with the
hatchet.
She went back into the kitchen carrying
the legs over her shoulder.

Nothing—and I mean nothing—

Had moved in there.

Between holes
In their own personal medications
Jake still babbled at Viva.

Viva still babbled at Jake.

"Oh quit your grinnin' and drop your linen,"
Jake spat at Viva.
Then reached into his leather bomber
jacket, over his skin-tight thermal
American flag Shirt, to wipe the
spit-globs off her face
With his snotty bandana.
His chin dropped again.

Viva didn't blink or flinch.

Delaney turned on her heel, and slammed
out, this time knife in hand.
She stabbed at the dumb carcass again
and again, until she had removed as
much meat as she could from the
hindquarter.

It was done.

Then?

She gave up.
What was left?
Only hanging on—
Those bones were
Demolished—
Of no use.
She, too, was done.

So she just sat there on the wooden steps—
next to the piles
Of dumped guts, skin, hooves, eyes.
And ears.

She took a long pull on her beer;
Finished it.

Her horizon was no more than a short
distance in any direction.
To the north were the back garage bays
of the "Beyond Repair" Auto Shop.
To the east, the ugly corrugated aluminum
wall of Rostrom's Shop.

And to the west, the broken piles of
windows stacked behind
The replacement window factory.
The south,
the big yellow whore house.

Nowhere to run.
She took the meat in her hands,
And carried it inside.

She pushed the pots of greens and
potatoes aside and began to cook up
the deer in the big cast iron skillet
always on the range.There was hardly
any room In the fridge, meaning most
of the deer had to be cooked now. What
she couldn't cook she put into a
garbage bag—two hind legs sticking
out.

She used the Heel of her black, steel-toed
engineer boot to cram it inside their
ancient blue fridge, shoving the hairy
legs on top of
The cases of beer.

Joe and Chili went out back to bury the
guts and bones.
Delaney checked out the kitchen scene
As she stirred the meat.

A Real Pilgrim Thanksgiving,
She mused.
*Everybody trying to hustle
somebody
But nobody getting over.*

Jake, usually the true master of SSI-Zen,
couldn't hustle Viva.
Delaney, obviously so much better than
Viva?

Couldn't hustle Jake.

Joe was too smart to try and hustle an
already-pissed-off Delaney,
Besides, his Run-Away Chick would be
back tomorrow if not tonight—
Joe had scruples. Just ask him.
"Nice guys finish last," was his motto.
And then Viva?

Well, Viva. . . well.
Wasn't saying much.

Ed sat. Drinking.
Macy primped.
Harry, the asshole, was busy berating Silver for being a bad mother.
Harry Jr. cried nonstop.

And Red-Neck? He was in and out of the bathroom.

Checking, just checking.

The turkey came out.
The potatoes were mashed,
Stuffing stuffed and unstuffed, green beans and mushroom soup crisped on top With fried onions punctuated with cranberry sauce, and stuffed peanut butter dates rolled in sugar—
a few stray joints—the whole package—laid out, garnished
With cases of beer, joints, and a good supply of Jack Daniels. Nobody really ate much.

It was done.

Nobody bothers with the leftovers,
She thought.

They all just sat there.
Full.
At one a.m. Delaney and Chili had had enough. They headed up to Buzzo to share the wealth—and get out of Pardee Street. They rode up Ashby, Chili thinking it was funny to go up and down every curb, while Delaney screamed on the back of the bike—her pack of meat, with the two left-over deer legs sticking out the top, kicking her in the head with each bump. They all played some music and passed out.

Except for Delaney.

She grabbed the bag of deer chunks and her jacket, and she left at about 2 am.

Berkeley in November.
Cold and wet, street-shining night—.

She was shivering in her "Ace Destruction"
Denim jacket.

I'm just a God-damned leftover,

She thought.

Berkeley—on the Ave—Again.

She had thought she had had it all figured—
But now she was back here—
As if she had never left.

That was how it was. Again.

Back here,
Because she had balked.
Her father and step-mother #1
Had tried to stick her into some
Uptown looney bin.

Oh-h-h, they had coaxed her.
James Taylor. He had been there.
Written some of His best stuff up there in
psych-ward Hippieland, in Stockbridge,
Massachusetts.
"Just Yesterday Morning. . . . "

There she was.
All tested up.
Beyond certifiable—
Professionally certified. Stamped.
Flunked out of the "real" world.

And then—with nowhere else to go,
She had accepted it.
Maybe they were right.
This life of hers was just not "normal."

Shit—Hadn't Mert,
Her 45-year-old ex—well, not-quite-yet
ex-brother-in-law—,
Hadn't He—almost blown her head off in
Tennessee
Just a few weeks ago? Yeah, well. . . and
Hadn't he thought "The Feds" were gonna
get him—for his crimes against
Mailboxes? Yeah. And then, when she
wouldn't agree to lure "The Feds"—

How she was supposed to lure
"The Feds" there
Had been more than a little fuzzy

But hadn't that been the plan for her?

Luring "The Feds" into the
Final ambush
Where Mert and Davy would be—
To take them out?— Hadn't
Barricades been
Erected? Yeah, but. . . .
Then—

When—she had refused?

Hey, shit, then

She had refused,

Hadn't he aimed
Right at her—Right at her head
And shot at her—
Point blank. His handy dandy little
  9mm automatic pistol aimed at her head,
And missed?
Sure
He had,
Just as sure as she'd fled out of that trailer
  house that she'd bought—when the
  commune had
Paid her to leave—dog under her arm—
New furniture and all—She had just

jumped—.But even then? It hadn't
ended at that.
Mert
Needed more.
He had still been so pissed that he hadn't
been able to shoot someone that he had
then shot
her then current husband (husband #2)
in the face with his shotgun instead—
mumbling—
Something about how—"'A course,"

He was
sorry, so sorry—but surely Davy? Davy
understood—Had to understand-
He loved him—but still
He had to understand that the point was:
Mert—just had to shoot
Someone.
I mean, Hell, he had only been out of prison
a few months—for another murder—
After all, wasn't his daddy
(now an 80-year-old man)
Still the local Justice of the Peace?
Peace?
And wouldn't Davy

Like him, Mert, to drive him to the hospital?
Davy nodded, spurting blood, he would.
"Yes."
That had happened, all right—and then,
  after securing both of them overnight in
  the Woodbury Courthouse drunk tank,
  with help from Mert's wife,
Delaney had taken their car.
She had driven it all the way to McMinnville
And parked it
Behind the bus depot.
She had cashed her and Davy's paychecks
  and had just enough
For a ticket
To the movies, and
For a bus ticket out.

She sat through 2 showings of James
  Caan in "Rollerball"
Until she and her dog split on the first bus
  heading East.

She'd headed
Toward
what passed for home.
Wasn't that normal?

So? Now, when it was all in the bag? They
had broken the news to her.
She was in. They smiled
(as if a mental hospital were a college).
She would be leaving for Massachusetts,
right way. Tomorrow—She was going—
Oh, but. . . one little thing:
No Dogs Allowed.
NO DOGS ALLOWED?

What the fuck? She thought.
Were they fucking kidding?
No Dogs?
The dog was the only shred of sanity left.
Leave the dog? Where? What?
How?

Obviously, she decided to leave town
instead.
Her first in a series to follow of
Stepmothers,
Black maid, pulled her aside.
"You ain"t crazy," she had said to
Delaney.
"They are."
Then she handed her a bag she had fixed—

A fried chicken, biscuits, apples, Oranges,
  and candy—
Pre-Thanksgiving feast.
She had then driven her to the bus station
Bought her a ticket.
Handing this greasy white girl the ticket
She couldn't afford to give her,
      "Go back to California.
      Never come back again."

Then the bus?
A trip—
Three days,
Almost four, non-stop—
And nights On Greyhound.
Jerking off across Nevada
With an illegal dog.

      She didn't give a shit.

Soldiers in uniform in the seats behind her—

      They didn't give a shit.

Slept past Winnemucca—Her Bored dog
Had crawled up under some asshole—
  who complained to the driver,

Who, in turn?

Didn't give a shit, either,

'Cause they changed drivers in Tahoe,
anyway,
So it wasn't his problem.

Coming down into reality, she looked
up
Into the cold night of the Berkeley
Hills
As the changing light shimmered
Green in the puddles.

Telegraph was empty as she walked up to
BJs.
Door was open and Joe's Run-Away Chick
hadn't been able to run away again yet
So there was a place to sleep.
Only thing was Jake and Lana, his
Run-Away Chick, were fucking so loud
that the loft was shaking.
Delaney and Joe gave up on sleep.

Tried moving—down to where the
Soon-to-be-bathroom was.

Where Luciano,
Some crazed, Illegal immigrant electrician,
who had been working under the delusion
that Anthony was actually
Gonna pay him,
Now pissed
The holidays were here—
And he, Luciano, had
Not been paid.

Take a number, Bub.

Luciano had shit on the pillow
Joe had hidden
Under some sheetrock—Joe laughed,
"Maybe he thinks it's some sort of organic
Invoice or something. Oh yeah, this is
gonna make Anthony pay."

But Anthony, the boss, was far from here,
Somewhere up in the nice part of town,
Above College, He was probably climbing
into bed
Right now. Or was already asleep, with his
tall blonde
bank teller lady friend—
No "Luciano Invoices" were reaching

Him tonight, or ever.
Sleep for Joe and Delaney?
Wasn't happening.
So Joe pulled out his stash, and the two of them made a pretty big dent in the half G of white, laughing themselves silly about Luciano, and Viva, and Jake. About Anthony and the Run-Away Chicks.

Finally, when the place stopped shaking, Joe and Delaney climbed back up into the sleeping loft, wading through the piles of tools, garbage, sheetrock, sheetrock dust, ripped bags of grout, tile cutters, tiles, broken, mismatches, empties and dog bowls, over, past the greasy hot plate.

They crashed on the mattress finally—
Expecting sleep.

Not to be.

Jake, now passed out for good, had started snoring.
Delaney climbed over him and straddled his legs backwards. With two hands she pulled his feet from the blankets.

She peeled off his gray socks from his pale,
  boiled-egg feet and stuffed them into his
  gaping mouth.
He didn't wake up,
But he didn't stop snoring, either.
She took the few chunks of meat from her
  backpack and threw them into the cold
Grease in the frying pan still on the hot
  plate.
They started to warm up.

"Thanksgiving."
She said, outloud, even though
Joe was now sleeping.
"Have some dinner," she said to no one,

Leftovers,
Always better the next day.

Without Eyes: Fueling Blindness

"Lord, do you not care that my sister has left me to get on with the work by myself? Tell her to come, lend a hand,"

But the Lord answered,

"Martha, Martha, You are fretting about so many things. But only one thing is necessary. The part Mary has chosen is best, and it shall not be taken from her."

—Luke 10: 38-42

Martha threw down the food.

"Screw you," she said. "Make your own supper and pay your own bail."

Wails.

The fairies are screaming in the
Woods tonight

As Bernadette gnaws off chunks of
Wabbit's back.
She chews on the small piece of his nose
that she has removed with her incisors.
He doesn't make a sound.
Only six people in the bar
But, still,
There is a fight.

Hiding. Out. Back,
Behind—
Izzy's Taxidermy Shop—
As instinctual as turning white in the
  winter—Many-Winters White.
"—Wabbit,"
I call out.
"Yeah," he whispers back.

As the cops come in through the door of
  Mr. Mike's Tavern and Pizza Parlor
  Emporium,
We slide around the building,
Following a sense-memory
Of other alley ways.   I feel him—
My way—his heart in my mouth—
Not beating, but burning.
"They took his gun," I whisper.
"Yeah" he said, "He was going to shoot
Izzy."
"Yeah! an' we took one offen him—last
time—
  the time when he only bit the end offen
Izzy's thumb."

Mr. Mike's shotgun is behind the bar

Loaded. Mr. Mike—5 feet of
  500 pounds of
Black-dyed leather and denim.
A Mister Is only in front
Of him—Behind
The bar—only Helen—
As in of Troy, NY, or some other shit hole—
As in the bartender
In contention as
Jimmy's ex—Izzy's
For the moment—

He is made
Maine

Maine-Girl—
  in her black corduroy pants and white shirt
Official—Maine-ironed,

Maine crying,

A Maine she-drunk.
"Jimmy gonna kill Izzy, he's crazy,
It's all my fault."
Wab shifted
As his face came into the light of the street
  lamp.

"I gotta key to Izzy's shop,"
He says.

Inside.
A half-stuffed baby bear.
Eyeless yet.
"Izzy told the guy
He couldn't,
He wouldn't.
Only a baby. Gee-zzz-ee,"
  said Wab, to comfort
Without having to acknowledge empty
  sockets—

Unseeing,
Unhearing,

With all those pieces—

Missing. Kai.

Kai. She
Used to be the one.
Back when it was jokes
And patched
And back when it was Jack—Daniels
And first choice was Cat—the beautiful

sister
And Schlitz Malt. Then came the coke—
The big flat smack,
but even then

Kai'd
Been
The one

Who called the ambulance
When Slim or Clyde,
Or Sleeping Bags Bob got the DTs
Too bad, or just the fits,
Too bad, so bad,
So bad, that everybody had to sit on him
And shove belts and empty wallets between gnashing green teeth

And thick, yellowed tongues.
Kai
Had been the one.
Then.
And when.
The cops had come.

When Wab still smiled
And made up names for himself

And places for himself,
And lives for himself, and for her—and then
for their kids.

She was there then.
When

They needed. Bail.
Or Cigarettes.
Or a ride with some straight people, to
Santa Rita.

Or to the next exit.
Back Exit Tonight.

Ghost Wabbit running in the blue-night
snow.
Behind the store of other-empty skins,
With his gimpy arm and the missing pieces
Of flesh, and the time-twisted legs
And the blankened eye.
There was only instinct left—to get up
The quarter to make the call—

Kai.
Kai: A frozen Iris—tapetum green
blaze

At the moment of impact—
When fear-iridescent—
Merges, becomes one.
With the smack of a headlight.—
Still night in the forest.
We warm our hands by that gullible
fire.

Back inside?
Jimmy and Izzy are hugging now, and crying
now—
And loving each other more than any fucking
woman—
More. Jimmy, Maine Always.
Daddy is Sheriff.
Izzy for the moment—Made Maine—
For the moment.
Like Adam—Made Holy—
By time and place (shot dead)
By another sheriff's son.

Inside. Gail and Mr. Mike dance to the
jukebox.
While the toothless five bum dollarless
drinks
From some other monetary plane. Bang.
Not the shot, just another gun.

This one in Jimmy's shoe—
Out the door—across the hood—
As if it were a state,
Izzy had him as if it were a country—
Izzy had him by the hair,
As if it were a continent.
Izzy had him—by the gun. . .
By the collar. . . .
Out of habit, I dance facing the door,
So I can see.

Him.
Wabbit. In the shadows,

Watching
Alone—Aware.
That Kai is now
Elsewhere—

In California, where—
When all the other marbles were blown from
  the circle
Becoming splintered cat's eyes in a jug,
Replacing empty sockets,
With more boys' games
Of splits and spins, with
The Mike-Spike she ached for—

A black-eyed special of bloody steak lips,
And broken arms.
And O.Ds and O.Ds,
But with Mister Karisma,
No! With Mr. Buddha-No-Knowledge
Sought by all meditators
On holy mountains, everywhere,
Well,

Now. She had him.
Her own personal Savior.
Her Martha arms finally stilled.

In casts.
On crutches—her teeth strung out
On dental floss, stitched to her once-sacred
Piss-tanned leather craft.
Some armored vest, or jacket—straight or

Full-metal,
Full Moon.
Over the snow.

The cops are back.
Wabbit and I fade into the past
Behind the bar—Beneath its homey, dirt-
yellowed-shadow.

While out front
Of Izzy's Taxidermy
They lead Jimmy away,
In handcuffs, bawling
"Baby-secure." Home: To "Daddy-Home."
As in "this very place"—
As in Maine.
As in. That unknown span of time,
Known to us, held. Filled.
Only in the remaining lives—
Mangled—in each other—

As—the other
Cop waits in this one-store town, for us,
To be real. . . .DWIs.
For us to go through. . . the signs,
The motions of putting finger
To nose.
On our way. To places.
That will never be
"Home."

"Gail, you drive. . . drive," I say.
Feeling like a shit, but fuck it.
Gail don't have a license to lose.
Or a name to go with it any more,
So there could be no real attachment to the

likes
Of DWIs.
But I? Now. No.
I can't risk it.
But—I can't stop the seeing of it.
Even. . . with only bloody sockets left,
I can't stop counting.   points—even
If it is only on fingers   or even stubs
of fingers
Stumbling to the car
I step on a piece of fur.

Mashed eyebrow in the dirty snow.
Izzy's.
Spit out by Jimmy.
But Izzy won't touch it now—
We all know that.
Some things?   They just ain't right—
Can't be sown.
Even with the best brand-name waxed
Dental floss.
Some flesh. Too friable.

I drive.
Gail propped up in the driver's seat,
Sporadically deciding—it's time to use the
pedals—

or not.
I am leaning over her,
I have always done for someone.

My job. Shit.

Wabbit don't drive. But
somehow he gets there.
At least the part of him that's not left—
Passed out and robbed beneath
A snow bank
Of broken snow—
Men

Women
Children. . . and I get up the next morning,
puking behind the pump-house.
Going out to the generator.
I reach for the line. It starts. We have water.
The light around me goes
To black and white—
A glossy picture,

Kai,
As she was.
A halo
Of lamp-post-mist above her head.

Kneeling in the wet-pavement—
florescence

Of pre-dawn
California: A Pan-handler's Altar
Of cold cement

Offering a Small Supplication
To the foggy chill
In the moment

Before she climbs into
The back of the ambulance.
To softly stroke
Clyde's lousy forehead,
As they pull out down Telegraph,
For Highland.

Back then.

Back when
We all could still feel
The cold

3.
Six-Dollar Tuesdays

Six-Dollar Tuesdays

It's a six-dollar Tuesday
In front of The Plasma Center

Gathering in
Teeth Chattering
Conversation.

Laid Out
In torn Naugahyde recliners

Avocado green
And Stumbling
Through the mandatory legal
  acknowledgements—
With last month's
Corner Junkie,
Now dressed up
In permanent press
White lab coat and shoes,
  as if.

As if
This somehow made it all
Professional.

As if
This were somehow now
Official.

Admitting to a name.
On a plastic bag
Of red cells.

About the Author

Annie Petrie-Sauter has written numerous stories and poems about the '60s and '70s. Her work has been published in three Bright Hill Press Anthologies, including the *Speaking the Words Anthology*, the *Word Thursdays Anthology*, and *Out of the Catskills and Just Beyond*, and by Maverick Press, Texas; in the *Berkeley Tribe;* and the *Rat Underground* newspapers. She is a poet of the performance variety and also has an interest in political essay and op-ed writing. Petrie-Sauter has been married for thirty years to Paul Sauter, a ceramics artist; they have two grown daughters.

About the Book

A Plastic Bag of Red Cells was designed by Bertha Rogers with cover art by the author, Annie Petrie-Sauter. The typeface for the cover and text is Adobe InDesign Folio Book Type. The book was printed on 60-lb. offset, acid-free, recycled paper in the United States of America. This first edition is limited to copies in paper wrappers.

About Bright Hill Press

OUR MISSION: To seek out, study, and collect the work of early and contemporary writers, storytellers, and artists, and to publish, disseminate, and present that work through publications and educational and public programs for the larger community.

OUR HISTORY: Bright Hill Press/Word Thursdays was founded in 1992 by Bertha Rogers, with the assistance of Ernest M. Fishman. A writer, teacher, and visual artist, Ms. Rogers serves as the organization's executive director and editor in chief. Mr. Fishman has served BHP as president and/or chief financial officer since its beginnings. Bright Hill Press is located at Bright Hill Literary Center, 94 Church Street, in the hamlet of Treadwell, in New York's Catskill Mountain Region; program participants are from Delaware, Otsego, Sullivan, Schoharie, Broome, and Chenango counties as well. Programs and services have grown to meet the stated and implied needs of both youth and adult populations in those counties, as well as the needs of the literary community in New York State and beyond. BHP's current administrative focus is on long-range planning, in order to better fulfill its mission and expand its programs.

OUR ARTISTIC PHILOSOPHY: Bright Hill Press is dedicated to increasing audiences' appreciation of the writing arts and oral traditions that comprise American literature, and to encouraging and furthering the tradition of oral poetry and writing in the Catskills. Writers and artists who participate in BHP's programs are selected for their artistic excellence, their ability and willingness to work within a community setting, and the diversity of their backgrounds, genres, and styles. BHP understands that recognition of the need for a literary community and a commitment to lifelong learning are critical aspects of audience development; the organization's programs for children and adults engender the spirit, craft, and imagination that make this possible.

OUR PROGRAMS are offered to people of all ages. Current program offerings include:

- Word Thursdays, a reading series begun in 1992 and presenting open readings followed by readings and discussion by featured authors;
- Bright Hill Books, publishing anthologies as well as poetry collections and chapbooks and interdisciplinary collections by individual authors since 1994;
- Bright Hill Library & Internet Wing, since 2004, a facility with more than 6,000 titles of prose and poetry, art, reference, nature, and children's books for the immediate and larger community;
- New York State's Literary Web Site, nyslittree.org (since 1999), and the New York State Literary Map (in print and online), developed and administered by BHP, in partnership with the New York State Council on the Arts;
- Word Thursdays Share the Words HS Poetry Mentoring Program and Competition, affording young poets a chance to write and present their own poetry in a public competition since 1996;
- Word Thursdays Literary Workshops for Kids &

Adults, offering, since 1994, innovative programs that celebrate and incorporate the elegant use of words with other disciplines;

- Word & Image Gallery, dedicated, since 2002, to presenting works by regional and national artists that integrate words and images;
- Patterns, BHLC's Literary Garden/Park for the whole community, landscaped and created by Catskill Outdoor Educational Corps, a program of Americorps at SUNY Delhi;
- BHLC Internship Program for College and HS Students, offering, since 1994, students an opportunity to learn the business of literature;

GOVERNANCE: Bright Hill Press/Word Thursdays is an independent 501 (c) (3), not-for-profit corporation governed by a board of directors representing the community the organization serves, and an advisory board from the larger community.

Bright Hill Press At Hand Poetry Chapbook Award Series

Haywire Rachel Contreni Flynn 2009 $10
(2007 Poetry Chapbook Award)
The Cut Worm Douglas Korb 2008 $8
(2006 Poetry Chapbook Award)
A Sense of Place Bhikshuni Weisbrot 2007 $8
(2005 Poetry Chapbook Award)
Gobbo: A Solitaire's Opera David Cappella 2006 $8
(2004 Poetry Chapbook Award)
Web-Watching Bruce Bennett 2005 $8
(2003 Poetry Chapbook Award)
Possum Shelby Stephenson 2004 $8
(2002 Poetry Chapbook Award)
First Probe to Antarctica Barry Ballard 2003 $8
(2001 Poetry Chapbook Award)
Inspiration Point Matthew J. Spireng 2002 $8
(2000 Poetry Chapbook Award)
What Falls Away Steve Lautermilch 2001 $8
(1999 Poetry Chapbook Award)
Whatever Was Ripe William Jolliff 1999 $8
(1997 Poetry Chapbook Award)
The Man Who Went Out for Cigarettes Adrian Blevins 1996 $8 (1995 Poetry Chapbook Award)

Bright Hill Press At Hand
Fiction Chapbook Award Series

Low Country Stories Lisa Harris $8
(1996 Fiction Chapbook Award)
Boxes Lisa Harris $8
(1998 Fiction Chapbook Award)

Bright Hill Press At Hand
Poetry Chapbook Series

A Plastic Bag of Red Cells
Annie Petrie-Sauter 2010 $10
Skunk Night Sonnets Daniel Waters 2009 $10
The Wooden Bowl Sharon Ruetenik 2009 $10
Love in the End Mary Kay Rummel 2008 $10
Effects of Sunlight in the Fog Alan Catlin 2008 $10
Picking Up Evelyn Duncan 2008 $8
The Lily Poems Liz Rosenberg 2008 $8
The Courtship and Other Tales
Kathryn Ugoretz 2007 $8
Hairpin Loop Anne Blonstein 2007 $8
The Coriolis Effect Michael Dowdy 2007 $8
It Does Not Julia Suarez 2006 $8
In Late Fields Steven Ostrowski 2006 $8
Instinct Joanna Straughn 2006 $8
Autobiography of My Hand Kurt S. Olsson 2006 $8
Degrees of Freedom Nicholas Johnson 2006 $8
Walking Back the Cat Lynn Pattison 2005 $8
The Spirit of the Walrus ElisaVietta Ritchie 2005 $8
LightsOut Tom Lavazzi 2005 $8
The Last Best Motif Naton Leslie 2005 $6

Bright Hill Press
Poetry Book Award Series

Raven's Paradise
Red Hawk 2010 $16

Infinite Beginnings
Lucyna Prostko 2009 $16
2007 Poetry Book Award
Chosen by Joan Larkin

How the Brain Grew Back Its Own History
Liz Beasley 2008 $14
2006 Poetry Book Award
Chosen by Jay Rogoff

Need-Fire
Becky Gould Gibson 2007 $14
2005 Poetry Book Award
Chosen by Liz Rosenberg

The Artist As Alice: From a Photographer's Life
Darcy Cummings 2006 $14
2004 Poetry Book Award
Chosen by Carolyne Wright

The Aerialist
Victoria Hallerman 2005 $12
2003 Poetry Book Award
Chosen by Martin Mitchell

Strange Gravity
Lisa Rhoades 2004 $12
2002 Poetry Book Award
Chosen by Elaine Terranova

The Singer's Temple
Barbara Hurd 2003 $12
2001 Poetry Book Award
Chosen by Richard Frost

Heart, with Piano Wire
Richard Deutch 2002 $12
2000 Poetry Book Award
Chosen by Maurice Kenny

My Father & Miro & Other Poems
Claudia M. Reder 2001 $12
1999 Poetry Book Award
Chosen by Colette Inez

Traveling Through Glass
Beth Copeland Vargo 2000 $12
1998 Poetry Book Award
Chosen by Karen Swenson

To Fit Your Heart into the Body
Judith Neeld 1999 $12
1997 Poetry Book Award
Chosen by Richard Foerster

Blue Wolves
Regina O'Melveny 1997 $12
1996 Poetry Book Award
Chosen by Michael Waters

My Own Hundred Doors
Pam Bernard 1996 $10
1996 Poetry Book Award
Chosen by Carol Frost

Bright Hill Press Poetry Book Series

Every Infant's Blood Graham Duncan 2002 $14.95
Flares and Fathoms Margot Farrington 2005 $14

Bright Hill Press Anthologies

Speaking the Words Anthology 1994 $6.95
The Word Thursdays Anthology of Poetry & Fiction 1995 $12.95
The Second Word Thursdays Anthology: Poetry & Prose by Bright Hill Press Writers
1999 $19.95

Bright Hill Press Word & Image Series

How Looking Becomes Seeing: Word Thursdays Youth Workshops Museum Research, Writing, & Visual Art Program
Edited by Bertha Rogers $16 (forthcoming)

A Special Mind, A Special Paw: The Art of Per Frykdahl
Edited by Bertha Rogers, with a Foreword by Nils Frykdahl $16 (forthcoming)

Breathing the Monster Alive
Eric Gansworth 2006 $16

On the Watershed: The Natural World of New York's Catskill Mountain Region/ Poetry & Prose by Catskill Student Writers
Edited by Bertha Rogers 2001 $14.95

Out of the Catskills & Just Beyond Literary & Visual Works by Catskill Writers & Artists
Edited by Bertha Rogers 1997 $24

Iroquois Voices, Iroquois Visions A Celebration of Contemporary Six Nations Arts
Edited by Bertha Rogers, with Maurice Kenny, Tom Huff, & Robert Bensen 1996 $15

Bright Hill Press Exhibition Series

Bright Hill Book Arts 2010 $16
Edited by Bertha Rogers
Juried by Elsi Vassdal Ellis & Bertha Rogers

Bright Hill Book Arts 2008 $16
Edited by Bertha Rogers
Juried by Keith Smith & Bertha Rogers

Bright Hill Book Arts 2007 $16
Edited by Bertha Rogers
With commentary by Karen Hanmer & Bertha Rogers

Bright Hill Book Arts 2006 $16
Edited by Bertha Rogers
With commentary by Richard Minksy & Bertha Rogers

Bright Hill Book Arts 2005 $16
Edited by Bertha Rogers
With commentary by Edward Hutchins & Bertha Rogers

Bright Hill Book Arts 2004 $12
Edited by Bertha Rogers
With commentary by Nancy Callahan & Louise Neaderland

Bright Hill Book Arts 2003 $10
Edited by Bertha Rogers
With commentary by Rory Golden & Keith Smith

Bright Hill Book Arts 2002 $10
Edited by Bertha Rogers
With commentary by Richard Minsky & Peter Verheyen

~ ~ ~

Ordering Bright Hill Press Books

BOOKSTORES & INDIVIDUALS: Bright Hill Press books are distributed to the trade and to the public by Small Press Distribution (spdbooks.com), 1814 San Pablo Ave., Berkeley, CA 94702-1624; Baker & Taylor, 44 Kirby Ave., POB 734, Somerville, NJ 08876-0734; and North Country Books (regional titles), 311 Turner St., POB 217, Utica, NY 13501-1727. Our books may also be found at
BarnesandNoble.com, Amazon.com, at your local bookstores, and at Bright Hill Press's website, brighthillpress.org (payment may be made by credit card or through PayPal). If your local bookstores do not stock Bright Hill Press books, please ask them to special order, or write to us at Bright Hill Press, POB 193, Treadwell, NY 13846-0193 or to our e-mail address: wordthur@stny.rr.com, or call at 607-829-5055. Further information may be found on our website: brighthillpress.org. Credit card orders may be placed at 607-829-5055.